SEA TURTLES

Heinemann Library
Chicago, Illinois

Elizabeth Laskey

Designed by Kimberly Saar, Heinemann Library
Illustrations and maps by John Fleck
Photo research by Bill Broyles
Originated by Ambassador Litho Ltd.
Printed by Wing King Tong in Hong Kong

07 06 05 04 03
10 9 8 7 6 5 4 3 2 1

Library of Congress Cataloging-in-Publication Data
Laskey, Elizabeth, 1961-
    Sea turtles / Elizabeth Laskey.
        p. cm. -- (Sea creatures)
Summary: Discusses the life of sea turtles, describing where they live, what they eat, how they behave, how humans study them, and what can be done to protect these creatures.
Includes bibliographical references (p.   ).
    ISBN 1-40340-962-5 (HC), 1-4034-3564-2 (pbk.)
    1. Sea turtles--Juvenile literature. [1. Sea turtles. 2. Turtles. 3. Endangered species.] I. Title. II. Series.
    QL666.C536 L368 200
    597.92--dc21
                        2002010623

Acknowledgments
The author and publishers are grateful to the following for permission to reproduce copyright material:

Cover photograph by Masa Ushioda/Seapics.com

Title page, pp. 4, 5, 6, 8, 9, 13, 15T, 16, 17, 18, 19B, 20, 23, 26, 27, icons Doug Perrine/Seapics.com; pp. 10, 28 David B. Fleetham/Visuals Unlimited; p. 11T Olivier Grunewald/Oxford Scientific Films; p. 11B Black Hills Institute of Geological Research, Inc.; p. 12 D. R. & T. L. Schrichte/Seapics.com; p. 14 David Kearnes/Seapics.com; p. 15B Larry Minden/Minden Pictures; p. 19T Roy David Farrig/Visuals Unlimited; p. 21 Julie Meech/Ecoscene/Corbis; p. 22 Norbert Wu Photography; p. 25 Kip Ross/National Geographic Society; p. 29 Rob & Ann Simpson/Visuals Unlimited

Special thanks to Daniel R. Evans, Education Coordinator, Caribbean Conservation Corporation (http://cccturtle.org) for his help in the preparation of this book.

Some words are shown in bold, **like this.** You can find out what they mean by looking in the glossary.

Contents

Where Would You Find a Sea Turtle?

You're standing on a beach in eastern India. It's early evening in late spring. In the shallow water near the shore, you see what looks like a bunch of greenish stones as big as bicycle tires. But they aren't stones. They are the shells of olive ridley sea turtles. The turtles are waiting for just the right moment to come ashore.

You raise your binoculars to get a better look. The sea turtles are moving! All along the edge of the beach a slow-moving army of them crawls toward you. One stops near you. It begins scooping up sand with its paddle-shaped **flippers.** Sand flies in all directions as the turtle digs a hole. Next, white eggs begin dropping out of the turtle. After laying about 100 eggs, the turtle stops, pushes sand over the hole, and slowly heads back to the sea.

As many as 100,000 olive ridley sea turtles nest at this beach in India each year.

What Kind of Creature Is a Sea Turtle?

Sea turtles are air-breathing **reptiles.** Sea turtles spend almost all of their time in the ocean.

This is a loggerhead sea turtle. It is the most common sea turtle found in the southeastern United States.

A reptile with a shell

All reptiles, including sea turtles, have dry, scaly skin. They breathe through lungs. They are also **cold-blooded.** This means that their blood matches the temperature of the water or air that surrounds them. Turtles are the only reptiles that have a shell. The tough shell on a turtle's back is one way it protects itself.

Sea turtles are good swimmers. Male sea turtles hardly ever go onto land. But females come up onto beaches to dig nests and lay eggs.

How Many Kinds of Sea Turtles Are There?

There are seven **species** of sea turtle. Different species have different features and live in different areas.

Olive ridley and Kemp's ridley sea turtles

The olive ridley and Kemp's ridley are the smallest sea turtle species. They are a lot alike. Both have heart-shaped, green-gray shells about 2 to 2.5 feet (61 to 76 centimeters) long. They weigh about 85 to 90 pounds (about 40 kilograms). Olive ridleys live in both the Pacific and Atlantic oceans as well as the Indian Ocean and the Caribbean Sea. The Kemp's ridley lives only in the eastern Atlantic Ocean.

Hawksbill sea turtles

The next largest sea turtle is the hawksbill. It has an oval shell that is about 2.5 feet (76 centimeters) long. It weighs about 120 pounds (54 kilograms). Hawksbills live in the Atlantic, Pacific, and Indian oceans. Hawksbills have very pretty brown-gold shells with streaks of white, green, red, and black in them.

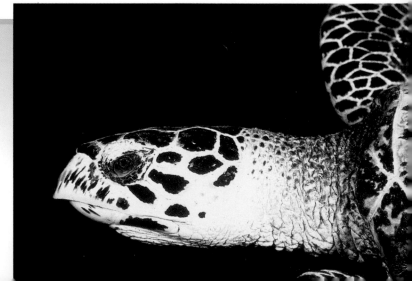

Hawksbills have a narrow and sharp upper jaw like the bill of a hawk.

6

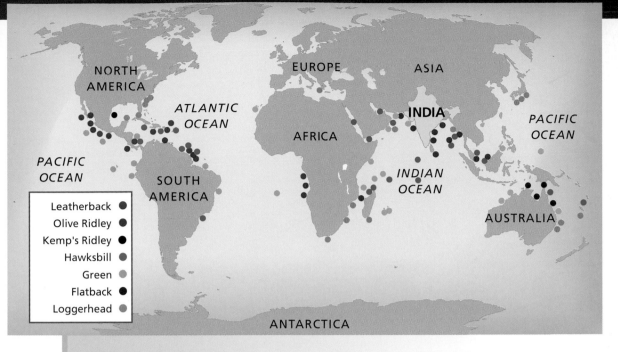

The colored dots show the major nesting sites of sea turtles around the world.

Flatback sea turtles

The flatback sea turtle is a bit larger than the hawksbill. It has a gray-green, oval shell that is about 3 feet (1 meter) long. Its shell is flatter than the shells of other species of sea turtles. It can weigh as much as 200 pounds (90 kilograms). Flatbacks live only in the shallow waters near the northern and northeastern coasts of Australia.

Loggerhead sea turtles

The loggerhead sea turtle is the next largest sea turtle after the flatback. Loggerheads have a reddish-brown oval shell that is about 3 to 3.5 feet (1 meter) long. They weigh about 300 pounds (136 kilograms). Loggerheads live in the Atlantic, Pacific, and Indian oceans and the Mediterranean and Caribbean seas.

Green sea turtles

The green sea turtle is the second-largest sea turtle. It has an oval-shaped shell that is about 3.5 to 4.5 feet (1 to almost 1.5 meters) long and weighs 350 to 500 pounds (160 to 230 kilograms). Green turtles are not named for the color of their shells, which is brown or black. They are called green sea turtles because their body fat is green. Green sea turtles live in the Atlantic, Pacific, and Indian oceans and the Mediterranean and Carribean seas.

Leatherback sea turtles

Leatherback sea turtles are the largest sea turtles. The leatherback can reach a length of 6 feet (1.8 meters) and weigh as much as 1,100 pounds (500 kilograms). Other sea turtles have hard shells, but leatherbacks have a soft, rubbery shell. The brown to black shell is teardrop-shaped, with some bony ridges running the length of the shell. Leatherbacks live in the Atlantic, Pacific, and Indian oceans. Sea turtles usually like to live in warmer waters. But leatherbacks do fine in water that is quite cold. Leatherbacks have been found as far north as Canada, where the water is only about 43 °F (6 °C).

The loggerhead turtle has a wide, square-shaped head and very powerful jaws.

How Is a Sea Turtle Different from a Land Turtle?

Sea turtles and land turtles look a lot alike. But there are important differences between the two.

The pattern of the leatherback's shell looks like long strips joined together.

A sea turtle can't hide in its shell

Land turtles and sea turtles both have shells. The top part of the shell is called the **carapace.** The bottom part is called the **plastron.** Openings between the carapace and the plastron are for the head, the legs, and the tail. Unlike a land turtle, a sea turtle cannot pull its head and legs inside its shell.

In hard-shelled sea turtles, the carapace and the plastron are made of bony plates that are joined together. The shiny **scutes** that cover the bony plates look like differently shaped tiles. Scutes are made from a strong, waterproof material called **keratin** that is also found in your fingernails. The leatherback's carapace is covered by tough, leathery skin instead of scutes.

A sea turtle has flippers instead of feet

Land turtles have legs and feet that help them walk on land. Sea turtles have two front **flippers** and two back flippers. The flippers are paddle-shaped. To swim, a sea turtle uses its front flippers like the oars of a rowboat. It reaches its flippers out in front and pulls them back close to its body. It uses its back flippers for steering and balance. Sea turtles glide easily through the water and can swim long distances. But on land the flippers are not very helpful. The shape of the flippers makes it hard for the sea turtles to walk. When on land, they push their heavy bodies slowly along with their flippers.

Green sea turtles like this one can swim as fast as 20 miles (32 kilometers) per hour. That's about as fast as an Olympic sprinter can run.

The leatherback sea turtle uses its jaws like scissors to snip food into pieces.

But some things are almost the same

Like land turtles, sea turtles can see, hear, and smell. Sea turtles see very well underwater. But on land it's hard for them to see things that are far away. Sea turtles don't have ears that you can see. Their eardrums are hidden by skin. Sea turtles have a nose with two nostrils. Scientists believe that sea turtles may use their sense of smell to find their way to the beaches where they nest. Sea turtles do not have teeth. But they have strong jaws and a hooked **beak** to catch and hold food.

Sea Turtles of the Past

One ancient sea turtle lived about 70 million years ago. It roamed Earth with dinosaurs such as *Tyrannosaurus rex*. From the tip of one front flipper to the other, the turtle was 20 feet (6 meters) wide—so wide it would barely fit into a two-car garage.

11

What Do Sea Turtles Eat?

Sea turtles eat many different sea animals and sea plants. Some **species** eat a wider variety of food than others.

Some sea turtles eat other sea animals

Hawksbills, flatbacks, leatherbacks, and olive and Kemp's ridleys eat other sea animals. They are **carnivores,** or meat eaters. Flatbacks like to eat shellfish and a long, skinny creature called a sea cucumber. Olive ridleys and Kemp's ridleys eat fish, crabs, and snails.

Hawksbill and leatherback sea turtles make very strange food choices. Hawksbills eat mainly sponges. They will even eat sponges that are poisonous to humans and sponges that have razor-sharp glass skeletons! Hawksbills eat spiky sea urchins and jellyfish, too. Leatherbacks eat mainly jellyfish.

? **Did you know?**

Each day, leatherbacks can eat an amount of jellyfish equal to their own body weight.

Leatherback sea turtles eat jellyfish-like creatures such as this Portuguese man-of-war. These creatures can give humans a painful sting that causes a bad rash, but Leatherbacks gobble them up without a problem.

Loggerheads use their powerful jaws to crush the shells of crabs, oysters, and queen conches like this one. They also use their jaws to pull and pry food away from the seafloor.

The green sea turtle mostly eats plants

Adult green sea turtles are mainly **herbivores,** or plant eaters. They have been known to eat a few sea animals such as sponges and jellyfish. But mostly they like to eat **seagrass** and seaweed.

Some sea turtles eat animals or plants

Some sea turtle species will eat animals or plants. These species are **omnivores.** Loggerheads and green turtles that are not fully grown are also omnivores. These two species eat algae, jellyfish, small shellfish, and sponges. When looking for food, loggerheads may poke around **coral reefs,** rocky areas, and even old sunken ships to find something tasty to eat.

What Do Sea Turtles Do?

Scientists are still learning the details of how sea turtles live when they are not on land. When they are out in the ocean, sea turtles divide their time between eating and resting. Sea turtles also swim long distances between **feeding grounds** and **nesting grounds.**

They eat a little, then rest a little

A sea turtle might look for food in the morning and then rest in the afternoon. When a sea turtle wants to rest, it may float to the surface. Green sea turtles in some areas, such as Hawaii, sometimes leave the water to **bask** on a **coral reef,** a beach, or a rock. They may do this to warm up in the sun, to rest, or to stay out of the way of sharks.

Some sea turtles dive to the bottom to rest. They can do this because they store oxygen in their blood and muscles. This lets them stay underwater for several hours before they need to come up to the surface to breathe.

It's not unusual for seabirds to perch on the back of a basking green sea turtle.

They swim long distances

Sea turtles may **migrate** hundreds or even thousands of miles to get from their feeding grounds to their nesting grounds. For example, some loggerheads cross the entire Pacific Ocean to get from nesting grounds in Japan to feeding grounds in Mexico. This is a distance of 7,500 miles (12,000 kilometers). It took one loggerhead six years to make this journey.

Other sea turtles don't migrate so far. A hawksbill might swim from the coast of Nicaragua to the coast of Jamaica, a distance of about 300 miles (500 kilometers).

Loggerhead nesting grounds in Japan.

 Did you know?

Green sea turtles can stay underwater for up to five hours.

Loggerheads that nest in Japan have been found at these feeding grounds in Baja, Mexico.

15

What Is Sea Turtle Family Life Like?

All sea turtles start their lives on land as eggs. Once hatched, the babies scramble toward the sea as fast as they can. Only a few make it to the sea and grow to be adults.

Females make nests and lay eggs

Every two to three years, female sea turtles return to the beach where they were born to nest. How they find the beach is still a mystery to scientists. One idea is that they use their sense of smell to guide them. Another is that they use Earth's magnetic fields to find their way.

When Kemp's ridleys and olive ridleys are ready to nest, hundreds or thousands of them storm the beach in a giant group. Other **species** go ashore to nest one-by-one or in small groups.

Olive ridley sea turtles may wait in the water for days before going up on the beach. Scientists think they are waiting for a signal that may have something to do with the phases of the moon or the strength of the wind.

A female digs a nest by scooping out sand with her back **flippers.** The finished nest is a hole that is usually wider at the bottom than the top.

Depending on the species, a female will lay about 80 to 120 eggs about the size of ping-pong balls. While laying the eggs, water trickles from the female's eyes. She is not crying. Special glands behind her eyes are getting rid of extra salt. The salt comes from the seawater that gets into her body through her nose and mouth when she is in the ocean.

Sea turtle eggs have soft shells.

She returns to the sea

After laying the eggs, the female covers the nest with sand. She rocks from side to side to pack it down. Then she uses her front flippers to mess up the sand and cover her tracks around the nest so **predators** won't find it.

Finally, she crawls back to the sea. She will not return to care for the eggs or the baby turtles. The eggs will develop on their own in the sun-warmed sand.

The eggs hatch

After about 60 days, the baby sea turtles, called **hatchlings,** begin breaking out of their eggs. If the nest was warm, above 85.1 °F (29.5 °C), most of the hatchlings will be female. If it was cooler, below 82.4 °F (28 °C), most of them will be males. If the temperature was somewhere in between, there will be a mix of females and males.

The hatchlings head for the sea

The hatchlings of most species wait until evening, when it is cooler, to leave the nest. Then they all pour out of the nest at the same time. They try to head for the ocean. Light from the moon or the sunset reflected on the water tells them which direction they should go. They hurry over the sand, but raccoons, wild pigs, seabirds, vultures, mongooses, jaguars, wild dogs, and other **predators** lie in wait to snap them up.

Kemp's ridley hatchlings move quickly to avoid ghost crabs. These crabs bury themselves in sand and then suddenly appear to attack and eat the hatchlings.

Frigate birds are predators of most species of sea turtle hatchlings.

The hatchlings grow up

Once in the sea, the hatchlings are still not safe. Sharks, fish, seagulls, and other birds may eat them. Only about 1 hatchling in 1,000 grows to adult size. The early years of sea turtles' lives are called "the lost years," because not much is known about this time of their lives. Scientists think that during this time, the young turtles live out in the open sea, drifting along in ocean currents.

Saving Eggs from Predators

Sea turtle eggs are often stolen out of nests by humans and by animal predators. In Rancho Nuevo, Tamaulipas, Mexico, where Kemp's ridley sea turtles nest, scientists move the eggs to nests in a safe, fenced area. When the eggs hatch, they take the hatchlings back to the nesting beach and put them safely into the sea. Since this program has been in place, the number of sea turtles nesting at Rancho Nuevo has increased.

19

Are Sea Turtles Endangered?

There were once many more sea turtles in the oceans than there are today. Hunting of sea turtles is one reason there are fewer turtles. Certain fishing methods and pollution also have killed many sea turtles. Today, all **species** of sea turtle except the flatback are listed as **endangered** by the International Union for the Conservation of Nature and Natural Resources (IUCN).

Hunting has killed many sea turtles

People hunt sea turtles and eat their meat and eggs. Many countries now have laws that protect endangered sea turtles. But hunting still goes on, legally and illegally. Egg stealing is a big problem. In 1996, for example, a truck filled with half-a-million stolen olive ridley eggs was caught in Mexico.

Hawksbill sea turtles have been hunted for their beautiful shells.

Sea turtles accidentally eat garbage on the beach such as pens, straws, bottle caps, cups, and other plastic items.

Crowded and polluted beaches are a danger

Many beaches where sea turtles nest now have hotels and other buildings on them. Lights from buildings cause problems for sea turtles. Sea turtles head toward light to find their way back to the ocean. On a dark beach, the brightest thing will be the ocean. Lights on the beach can confuse sea turtles and make them head in the wrong direction. This is especially bad for **hatchlings.** The more time they spend wandering on the beach, the more likely it is they will be eaten by a **predator.**

Garbage on beaches and in the water is also a problem. Sea turtles sometimes think plastic bags or empty helium party balloons floating in water are jellyfish and eat them. These items clog a turtle's digestive system and can kill the turtle.

21

Fishnets and lines can kill sea turtles

Trawl nets used by shrimp fishing boats accidentally kill more sea turtles than any other fishing method. A trawl net is a funnel-shaped net that is pulled behind a boat. Sea turtles swim into the net and get trapped. They cannot get to the surface to breathe, so they drown. As many as 150,000 may die in trawl nets each year.

Longline fishing kills about 40,000 sea turtles a year. A longline can be up to 60 miles (96 kilometers) long, with as many as 3,000 hooks on it. Longlines are used to catch swordfish and tuna, but sea turtles often eat the bait on longline hooks. The hooks get stuck in their mouth or throat, which can kill them. They can also get tangled in the lines and then they cannot get to the surface to breathe. Huge **driftnets** that stretch for miles have also killed thousands of sea turtles.

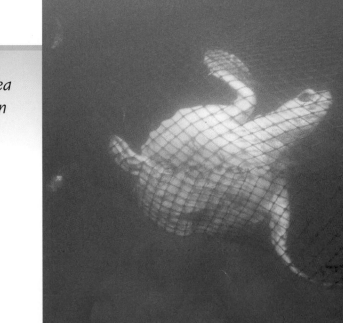

This hawksbill sea turtle drowned in this fishing net.

What Can We Do to Save Sea Turtles?

Laws are in place in many nations and regions to help protect sea turtles and their **habitat.** Fishermen have also made changes so that fewer sea turtles are accidentally caught.

Laws can protect sea turtles

Many nations have laws to protect **endangered** sea turtles that live in their waters. These laws make it illegal to kill or hurt endangered sea turtles or take their eggs. Countries that have laws like this include the United States, Costa Rica, and Australia. These laws also usually call for the government to make plans to help the **species** increase their numbers.

The IUCN does not list the flatback as endangered. But the flatback and all other species of sea turtle are protected by law in Australia.

In addition, there is a worldwide law against the buying and selling of any sea turtle products. People who break any of these laws may be **fined** or even sent to prison.

We can change how we fish

Many governments make their shrimp fishermen fit their nets with a **Turtle Excluder Device (TED).** A TED makes a "trap door" in a shrimp **trawl net** so that a turtle can escape if it gets caught. Almost all turtles caught in a net with a TED escape. But not all countries use them.

In 1992, the United Nations passed a ban on using huge **driftnets** in the open sea. This may have saved many sea turtles from drowning. Many people are asking for the same kind of law against **longline fishing.** It has already been banned along the coast of Florida.

We can set up safe places for sea turtles

Protecting the feeding and nesting **habitat** of sea turtles is very important. In South Africa, leatherbacks and loggerheads can nest safely at the Greater St. Lucia Wetland Park. The Ningaloo Marine Park in Australia is a protected **coral reef** area where loggerhead, green, and hawksbill turtles can find food and quiet nesting beaches.

When a sea turtle hits the metal bars of the TED in the trawl net, the "trap door" opens and the turtle can escape.

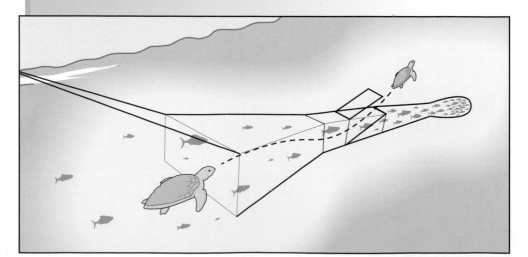

Archie Carr in 1961 with baby sea turtles. In 2000 more than 2,800 green sea turtles nested at the Archie Carr National Wildlife Refuge.

The Archie Carr National Wildlife Refuge in Florida was set up in 1989 so that sea turtles would have a safe place to nest. More loggerhead turtles nest there than anywhere else in the world. Green and leatherback turtles also nest there.

Archie Carr (1907-1987)

Archie Carr grew up in Savannah, Georgia, where he had pet lizards, snakes, and turtles. As a young man he worked as a scientist in Honduras in Central America. One day he saw a sea turtle nesting. He decided he must find out more about these interesting creatures. In the 1950s, he and his family went to Costa Rica, where many green sea turtles nest. Carr became the first expert on sea turtles. He also spoke out about the need to protect sea turtles. He founded the Caribbean Conservation Corporation (CCC) in 1959. Carr helped set up protected areas for sea turtles, like Tortuguero National Park in Costa Rica. Today, CCC and many others carry on the work Archie Carr began.

25

How Do We Learn About Sea Turtles?

It is not easy to study sea turtles because they do not spend much time on land. **Technology** has made it easier for scientists to find out more about how sea turtles migrate and how they act in the ocean.

Scientists put tags on sea turtles

When sea turtles come on shore, scientists collect **data** about the turtles' size and other features. Then they put metal tags on two of the turtle's **flippers.** The tags don't bother the turtle at all. Each tag has a number on it and a note. The note asks anyone who finds the tag to return it to the scientists. When a tag is returned, scientists learn important information about where the sea turtle traveled after it left the nesting beach where it was tagged.

Scientists may put tags on the back or the front flippers.

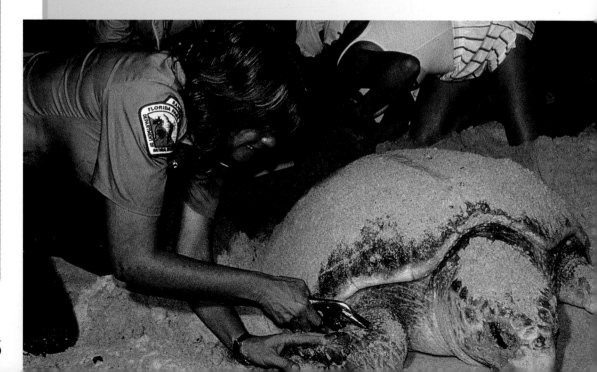

Transmitters also send data about water temperature and about how often a sea turtle dives.

Scientists track sea turtles with satellites

Scientists can also track sea turtle **migrations** from space by gluing a **transmitter** to a sea turtle's shell. When the sea turtle comes to the surface, the transmitter sends a signal that can be picked up by a **satellite** above the Earth. The satellite then sends data about the sea turtle's location back to the scientists. Scientists use this data to build a picture of the path a sea turtle takes when it migrates.

Satellite tracking can have a sad ending. A green sea turtle named Miss Junie nested in Costa Rica in September 2000. Scientists tracked her as she swam north. Signals from Miss Junie stopped in August 2001. She had been killed by a fisherman in Nicaragua, where some sea turtle hunting is still allowed. The news reminded people that sea turtles are world travelers. If sea turtles are to have a future, protection needs to be a worldwide effort so that the turtles will be safe in all the waters they travel through.

- One loggerhead sea turtle had a head that was 10 inches (27 centimeters) wide. That's about the size of a dinner plate.

- So many olive ridleys come ashore at once, that some of them accidentally dig up other olive ridley nests when they start digging their own.

Green turtles off the coast of Hawaii don't seem to be afraid of people and will join them on diving trips.

- Leatherback turtles make a variety of sounds while they are nesting, ranging from sighs to burps.

- Sea turtles have lived on Earth millions of years longer than humans.

- Leatherbacks can get mad. Scientists once watched a leatherback chase a shark that had attacked it. When the shark was safely out of the way, the leatherback tried to attack the boat the scientists were on!

- Loggerheads may spend 85 percent of their time underwater.

- Only about half of a leatherback's eggs hatch. The eggs that don't hatch are either too small or don't have enough yolk. Scientists think that the eggs that don't hatch might serve as spacers to keep the eggs that will hatch from being too close together.

The beach in Mexico where the highly endangered Kemp's ridley sea turtle nests is protected by armed guards.

The biggest sea turtle ever measured was a male leatherback that washed ashore in Wales, which is part of Britain. It was 8.4 feet (2.5 meters) long and weighted 2,020 pounds (916 kilograms). That's about the same weight as 12 refrigerators!

A green sea turtle's heart can slow down to one beat every nine minutes. The human heart beats at least 550 times in nine minutes.

Kemp's ridley sea turtles are the most endangered of all sea turtles, but they seem to be slowly increasing their numbers. In 1985, only about 300 females came ashore to nest. By the late 1990s, the number had increased to about 1,700.

Leatherback turtles have a pink spot on the top of their heads. Each pink spot is different, like a human fingerprint.

Glossary

bask to warm up in the sun

beak hooked top part of a sea turtle's jaw

carapace top part of a sea turtle's shell

carnivore animal that eats other animals

cold-blooded having blood that is the same temperature as the air or water an animal lives in

coral reef underwater formations made of the hard skeletons of millions of tiny sea animals

data facts and information

driftnet large fish net that may stretch for miles

endangered in danger of dying out

feeding grounds area where sea turtles go to find food

fined made to pay an amount of money for breaking the law

flippers paddle-shaped front and back legs

habitat place where an animal lives in the wild

hatchling baby sea turtle that has just hatched from an egg

herbivore eats plants

keratin strong, waterproof material that covers the bony plates of a hard-shelled turtle's shell. Keratin is also found in human fingernails and hair.

longline fishing way of fishing that uses a very long line with many hooks

migrate move from one place to another

migration act of moving from one place to another

nesting grounds area where sea turtles mate and build nests

omnivore animal that eats plants and animals

plastron bottom part of a sea turtle's shell

predator animal that hunts and eats another type of animal

reptile cold-blooded animal with scaly skin that breathes through lungs

satellite object launched into orbit around Earth that can receive information and send it back to Earth

scutes shiny, tile-shaped coverings over the bony plates of a hard-shelled turtle's shell

seagrass grassy underwater plant

species group of animals that have the same features and can have babies with each other

technology use of information about a subject to accomplish a task

transmitter something that sends out signals

trawl net funnel-shaped fishnet that is dragged behind a boat

Turtle Excluder Device (TED) "trap door" in a shrimp trawl net that lets a sea turtle escape from the net if it gets caught

More Books to Read

Dunbier, Sally. *Sea Turtles*. Hauppauge, N.Y.: Barrons Juveniles, 2000.

Rustad, Martha E.H. *Sea Turtles*. Bloomington, Minn.: Pebble Books, 2001.

Sayre, April Pulley. *Turtle, Turtle, Watch Out!* Danbury, Conn.: Orchard Books, 2000.

Index